The Ultimate Gluten-Free Air-Fryer Cookbook 2023

Unleash the Power of Air Fryer Cooking with 35 Delicious, Quick & Easy Recipes for Optimal Health

By

Dr. John A. Roberts

Copyright © 2023 John Roberts

All rights reserved. No part of this publication may be reproduced, distributed, or transmitted in any form or by any means, including photocopying, recording, or other electronic or mechanical methods, without the prior written permission of the publisher, except in the case of brief quotations embodied in critical reviews and certain other noncommercial uses permitted by copyright law.

Table of Contents

INTRODUCTION..5
CHAPTER ONE..11
The Fundamentals of Air Frying: Mastering the Techniques for Perfect Results..................................11
CHAPTER TWO..17
Essential Kitchen Tools and Ingredients for Gluten-Free Air Fryer Cooking..................................17
    Kitchen Tools:..................................17
    Gluten-Free Ingredients:..................................19
CHAPTER THREE..23
Wholesome Mornings: Breakfast and Brunch Creations to Kick-Start Your Day..................................23
    Crispy Bacon and Egg Cups..................................23
    Crunchy Granola Clusters..................................24
    Stuffed Avocado with Eggs..................................25
    Cinnamon Apple Chips..................................27
    Spinach and Feta Egg Muffins..................................28
CHAPTER FOUR..31
Crispy Bites: Appetizers and Snacks for Gluten-Free Delights..................................31
    Crispy Chickpea Snack..................................31
    Mozzarella Sticks..................................32
    Crispy Brussels Sprouts..................................33
    Chicken Wings..................................34
    Sweet Potato Chips..................................35
CHAPTER FIVE..37
Sizzling Sensations: Flavorful Gluten-Free Meats and Seafood..................................37
    Lemon Herb Salmon..................................37
    Spicy Chicken Drumsticks..................................38
    Garlic and Herb Turkey Meatballs..................................39
    Coconut Shrimp..................................41
    Honey Mustard Glazed Pork Chops..................................42
CHAPTER SIX..45
Veggie Delights: Elevating Gluten-Free Vegetables to New Heights..................................45

  Roasted Brussels Sprouts..45
  Zucchini Fries...46
  Sweet Potato Fries...47
  Parmesan Roasted Cauliflower..48
  Eggplant Chips...49

CHAPTER SEVEN..51
 Comfort Classics Reinvented: Gluten-Free Air Fryer Makeovers...51
  Crispy Cauliflower Buffalo Wings..51
  Quinoa-Crusted Chicken Tenders..52
  Baked Zucchini Fries..54
  Sweet Potato Tots...55
  Eggplant Parmesan..57

CHAPTER EIGHT...61
 International Flavors: Exploring Gluten-Free Air Fryer Recipes from Around the World..61
  Korean-Style Chicken Wings...61
  Mexican-Style Stuffed Peppers..62
  Thai-Style Coconut Shrimp..65
  Indian-Style Vegetable Samosas..66
  Japanese-Style Teriyaki Salmon..68

CHAPTER NINE...71
 Sweet Indulgences: Irresistible Gluten-Free Desserts and Treats..71
  Cinnamon Sugar Donut Holes...71
  Berry Crumble Bars...72
  Chocolate Chip Cookies...74
  Apple Hand Pies...76
  Vanilla Glazed Donuts..78

CHAPTER TEN..81
 Bonus: Tips, Tricks, and Modifications for Gluten-Free Air Frying Success...81

CONCLUSION...87

INTRODUCTION

Nancy, a vibrant and adventurous woman, discovered a whole new world of flavor and health when she embraced gluten-free air-fryer dishes. Tired of feeling limited by her gluten intolerance, she took matters into her own hands and embarked on an exciting culinary journey.

With her trusty air fryer as her partner in the kitchen, Nancy fearlessly explored new recipes and experimented with a variety of gluten-free ingredients. She flipped, tossed, and seasoned her way to mouthwatering creations, each one more satisfying than the last.

From crispy chicken tenders to perfectly roasted vegetables, Nancy's dishes showcased her creativity and passion. Her friends and family marveled at the irresistible aromas and flavors that emerged from her kitchen. They couldn't believe that gluten-free cooking could be so indulgent and enjoyable.

Word of Nancy's gluten-free air-fryer dishes spread like wildfire. Soon, she found herself sharing her recipes and tips with others who were seeking delicious alternatives to traditional gluten-filled meals. Nancy's journey not only transformed her own life but also inspired countless individuals to embrace a gluten-free lifestyle without sacrificing taste or texture.

As Nancy continues to explore new possibilities in her kitchen, she remains a shining example of how determination and a little culinary creativity can open doors to a world of mouthwatering and gluten-free delights. Her journey reminds us all that with the right tools and a dash of passion, we can turn any dietary restriction into an opportunity for culinary magic.

Embracing a gluten-free lifestyle can be a transformative journey, and when combined with the convenience and deliciousness of air fryer cooking, it becomes an even more incredible experience.

For individuals with gluten intolerance or those simply opting for a gluten-free diet, the air fryer becomes a powerful tool in their culinary arsenal. It allows them to enjoy crispy and flavorful dishes without compromising their dietary needs.

Air fryers use hot air circulation to create a crispy texture with minimal oil, making them ideal for gluten-free cooking. From perfectly golden chicken tenders to crispy vegetable chips, the air fryer can achieve that satisfying crunch that was once off-limits to those avoiding gluten.

Not only does air frying offer a healthier alternative to traditional frying methods, but it also opens up a world of culinary possibilities. With a gluten-free lifestyle, one can explore a myriad of ingredients and flavors, creating unique and exciting dishes. The air fryer becomes a versatile companion, transforming gluten-free ingredients into culinary masterpieces.

By embracing a gluten-free lifestyle with air fryer cooking, individuals can reclaim their love for food. They can savor the pleasure of indulgent treats like crispy fries, crunchy onion rings, and even delectable desserts—all gluten-free and bursting with flavor.

Furthermore, air fryer cooking is convenient and time-saving, allowing busy individuals to whip up quick and nutritious meals with ease. The air fryer's efficiency and versatility make it an invaluable asset in the pursuit of a gluten-free lifestyle.

So, whether you're a gluten-free veteran or just starting your journey, embrace the power of air fryer cooking. Discover the joy of creating gluten-free meals that are both healthy and scrumptious. The combination of a gluten-free lifestyle and the magic of air fryer cooking opens up a world of culinary delights and empowers you to savor every bite without compromise.

CHAPTER ONE

The Fundamentals of Air Frying: Mastering the Techniques for Perfect Results

The culinary world has been swept up by air frying, which provides a healthier alternative to conventional frying techniques. The technique relies on hot air circulation to create a crispy texture, all while using minimal or no oil. Whether you're new to air frying or looking to enhance your skills, mastering the fundamentals is crucial for achieving perfect results every time. In this guide, we'll explore the key techniques and tips to help you become an air frying maestro.

Get to Know Your Air Fryer:
Start by familiarizing yourself with the features and functions of your air fryer. Each model may have specific settings and temperature ranges, so take the

time to read the manual and understand its capabilities. This knowledge will serve as the foundation for your air frying journey.

Preheating:

Preheating your air fryer is essential to ensure consistent cooking and optimal results. Most air fryers have a preheat function, which allows the appliance to reach the desired temperature before adding your ingredients. This step ensures even cooking and helps achieve that coveted crispy texture.

Choosing the Right Oil (or Not):

While air frying requires significantly less oil compared to traditional frying, some recipes may still benefit from a light coating. Opt for oils with high smoke points, such as avocado oil, canola oil, or grapeseed oil. Alternatively, you can skip the oil altogether and rely on the natural fats and moisture in your ingredients for cooking. Experiment with both methods to find what works best for each recipe.

Properly Seasoning:

Seasoning is key to enhancing the flavor of your air-fried creations. Whether it's a sprinkle of salt, a blend of herbs and spices, or a marinade, ensure your ingredients are well-seasoned before placing them in the air fryer. This step ensures that every bite is packed with deliciousness.

Proper Placement and Spacing:

For even cooking, it's important to arrange your ingredients in a single layer, leaving enough space for the hot air to circulate. Overcrowding the basket can result in uneven cooking and prevent that desired crispiness. If necessary, cook in batches to maintain proper spacing and ensure perfect results.

Flipping and Shaking:

During the cooking process, remember to flip or shake your ingredients. This makes sure that all the sides get an equal amount of browning and crispness. Use tongs or a spatula to gently turn over your food or give the basket a shake to redistribute the ingredients. Just be cautious not to overcrowd or lose any ingredients in the process.

Monitoring Cook Times:
Keep a close eye on the cooking time for each recipe, as air fryers tend to cook food faster than traditional methods. Set a timer and periodically check on your ingredients to avoid overcooking. It may take a few tries to find the perfect timing for your preferred level of crispness, but practice makes perfect.

Adding Moisture:
For certain dishes, adding a touch of moisture can prevent drying out. Consider spritzing a little water or oil on ingredients that tend to become dry, such as chicken breasts or delicate vegetables. This helps retain moisture and ensures a juicy and tender result.

Experiment and Adapt:

Air frying opens up a world of culinary possibilities, so don't be afraid to experiment. Adjust cooking times and temperatures, play with different seasonings, and try out various ingredients to create unique and delicious dishes. Embrace the versatility of air frying and let your creativity soar.

By mastering these fundamentals of air frying, you'll be well on your way to achieving perfect results in your culinary creations. Remember, practice and experimentation are key to becoming an air frying maestro. So grab your air fryer, gather your ingredients, and embark

CHAPTER TWO

Essential Kitchen Tools and Ingredients for Gluten-Free Air Fryer Cooking

Embarking on a gluten-free air fryer cooking journey can be both exciting and rewarding. To ensure successful and delicious results, it's essential to have the right tools and ingredients at your disposal. In this guide, we'll explore the must-have kitchen tools and ingredients that will elevate your gluten-free air frying experience.

Kitchen Tools:

Air Fryer: Of course, the star of the show is the air fryer itself. Choose a model that suits your needs, whether it's a countertop version or an oven with air frying capabilities. Look for features like adjustable temperature controls, timer settings, and a spacious cooking basket. Consider the size of your household and the amount of food you plan to cook to select the right capacity for your air fryer.

Mixing Bowls: Various sizes of mixing bowls are indispensable for preparing ingredients, marinating, and tossing seasonings. Opt for stainless steel or glass bowls, as they are durable and easy to clean.

Measuring Cups and Spoons: Precise measurements are crucial in gluten-free cooking. A set of measuring cups and spoons ensures accurate proportions, especially when working with gluten-free flours and other ingredients.

Tongs and Spatulas: Tongs and spatulas are handy tools for flipping, turning, and removing food from the air fryer. Look for heat-resistant and non-scratch materials to protect the coating of your air fryer basket.

Baking Sheets and Parchment Paper: Some air fryer models come with accessories like baking sheets or trays. These can be useful for baking or roasting ingredients. Parchment paper is also handy for lining the air fryer basket, preventing sticking and making cleanup easier.

Food Thermometer: A food thermometer is essential for ensuring that proteins, such as chicken or meat, reach the appropriate internal temperature for safe consumption. This tool helps prevent undercooking or overcooking.

Wire Rack: A wire rack allows air to circulate around food during cooking, promoting even browning and crispness. It's particularly useful for air frying breaded or coated items.

Gluten-Free Ingredients:

Gluten-Free Flours: Stock up on a variety of gluten-free flours, such as almond flour, coconut flour, rice flour, or gluten-free all-purpose flour blends. These flours serve as substitutes for wheat flour in recipes, allowing you to create delicious gluten-free versions of your favorite dishes.

Gluten-Free Grains: Include a range of gluten-free grains in your pantry, such as quinoa, rice (both white and brown), millet, and gluten-free oats. These grains provide versatility and can be used as side dishes, in salads, or as ingredients in gluten-free baked goods.

Gluten-Free Breads and Wraps: Gluten-free bread and wraps are essential for making sandwiches, wraps, or toasting for a crispy accompaniment. Look for options made from gluten-free grains and natural ingredients.

Fresh Fruits and Vegetables: Load up on fresh produce to incorporate into your gluten-free air fryer dishes. Fruits and vegetables add flavor, color, and nutrition to your meals. Explore a variety of options, including leafy greens, root vegetables, berries, and citrus fruits.

Gluten-Free Proteins: Choose high-quality, gluten-free proteins such as chicken, turkey, fish, beef, pork, and tofu. Ensure that they are free from gluten-containing marinades, seasonings, or coatings.

Gluten-Free Condiments and Seasonings: Gluten can often hide in condiments and seasonings, so be mindful of your choices. Opt for gluten-free alternatives of soy sauce, Worcestershire sauce, BBQ sauce, and salad dressings. Additionally, stock up on gluten-free spices, herbs, salt, and pepper to season your dishes to perfection.

Nuts, Seeds, and Nut Butters: Incorporate a variety of gluten-free nuts, seeds, and nut butters into your cooking. They add texture, flavor, and healthy fats to your gluten-free recipes. Almonds, walnuts, chia seeds, flaxseeds, and almond butter are excellent options.

Gluten-Free Sweeteners: For those with a sweet tooth, have gluten-free sweeteners on hand. These include honey, maple syrup, agave nectar, and coconut sugar. They can be used in baking, dressings, marinades, and sweet treats.

By equipping your kitchen with these essential tools and ingredients, you'll be well-prepared to embark on a successful gluten-free air frying journey. Enjoy the freedom to explore new recipes, flavors, and textures while maintaining a gluten-free lifestyle. With practice and creativity, you'll be whipping up delicious gluten-free air fryer meals that are both healthy and satisfying. So, gather your tools, stock your pantry, and let the gluten-free air frying adventure begin!

CHAPTER THREE

Wholesome Mornings: Breakfast and Brunch Creations to Kick-Start Your Day

Crispy Bacon and Egg Cups

Ingredients:

- 6 slices of bacon
- 6 large eggs
- Salt and pepper, to taste
- Chopped fresh chives (optional, for garnish)

Instructions:

- Preheat your air fryer to 350°F (175°C).
- Line each cavity of a muffin tin with a slice of bacon, forming a cup shape.
- Crack one egg into each bacon cup, being careful not to break the yolk.
- Season with salt and pepper.

- Place the muffin tin in the air fryer basket and cook for 10-12 minutes until the eggs are cooked to your desired level of doneness.
- Carefully remove the bacon and egg cups from the air fryer and let them cool slightly.
- Garnish with chopped fresh chives, if desired, and serve hot.

Crunchy Granola Clusters

Ingredients:
- 1 cup gluten-free rolled oats
- 1/2 cup chopped nuts (e.g., almonds, walnuts, or pecans)
- 1/4 cup unsweetened shredded coconut
- 2 tablespoons honey or maple syrup
- 1 tablespoon coconut oil
- 1/2 teaspoon vanilla extract
- 1/4 teaspoon ground cinnamon
- Pinch of salt

Instructions:

- In a mixing bowl, combine the oats, chopped nuts, shredded coconut, cinnamon, and salt.
- Melt the coconut oil over low heat in a small saucepan. Add the honey (or maple syrup) and vanilla extract, stirring until well combined.
- Pour the liquid mixture over the dry ingredients and stir until all the ingredients are evenly coated.
- Transfer the mixture to the air fryer basket and spread it out in an even layer.
- Air fry at 300°F (150°C) for 10 minutes, then carefully stir the mixture.
- Continue air frying for an additional 5-10 minutes until the granola clusters are golden brown and crisp.
- Remove from the air fryer and let cool completely before breaking into clusters. Store in an airtight container.

Stuffed Avocado with Eggs

Ingredients:

- 2 avocados
- 4 eggs
- Salt and pepper, to taste
- Fresh herbs (e.g., parsley or chives), for garnish

Instructions:

- Preheat your air fryer to 375°F (190°C).
- Remove the pits from the avocados by cutting them in half lengthwise.
- Use a spoon to scoop out a bit of flesh from each avocado half, creating a well for the egg.
- The avocado halves should be placed in the air fryer basket.
- Crack one egg into each avocado half, being careful not to overflow.
- Season with salt and pepper.
- Air fry for 10-12 minutes until the egg whites are set and the yolks are cooked to your desired level of doneness.
- Remove from the air fryer and garnish with fresh herbs.

- Serve immediately.

Cinnamon Apple Chips

Ingredients:
- 2 apples (such as Granny Smith or Honeycrisp)
- 1 teaspoon ground cinnamon
- 1 tablespoon honey or maple syrup (optional)

Instructions:
- Thinly slice the apples into rounds, removing the core and seeds.
- In a mixing bowl, toss the apple slices with cinnamon and honey (or maple syrup), if using, until evenly coated.
- In the air fryer basket, arrange the apple slices in a single layer.
- Air fry at 375°F (190°C) for 8-10 minutes, flipping the slices halfway through, until they are crispy and golden.
- Remove from the air fryer and let cool completely before enjoying as a crunchy

gluten-free snack or topping for yogurt or oatmeal.

Spinach and Feta Egg Muffins

Ingredients:
- 6 large eggs
- 1 cup packed fresh spinach, chopped
- 1/4 cup crumbled feta cheese
- 1/4 cup diced red bell pepper
- Salt and pepper, to taste

Instructions:
- Preheat your air fryer to 350°F (175°C).
- Whisk the eggs until well beaten, in a mixing bowl.
- Add the chopped spinach, crumbled feta cheese, diced red bell pepper, salt, and pepper to the bowl. Mix everything up thoroughly.
- Fill each muffin cup with about two-thirds of the mixture as you spoon it into the oiled cups.

- Place the muffin tin in the air fryer basket and cook for 12-15 minutes until the egg muffins are set and slightly golden.
- Remove from the air fryer and let cool for a few minutes before removing the muffins from the tin.
- Serve warm as a delicious and nutritious gluten-free breakfast option.

CHAPTER FOUR

Crispy Bites: Appetizers and Snacks for Gluten-Free Delights

Crispy Chickpea Snack

Ingredients:
- 1 can chickpeas, drained and rinsed
- 1 tablespoon olive oil
- 1 teaspoon ground cumin
- 1/2 teaspoon paprika
- 1/2 teaspoon garlic powder
- Salt and pepper, to taste

Instructions:
- Preheat your air fryer to 400°F (200°C).
- Pat-dry the chickpeas with a paper towel to remove excess moisture.
- In a bowl, toss the chickpeas with olive oil, cumin, paprika, garlic powder, salt, and pepper until well coated.

- The seasoned chickpeas should be placed in the air fryer basket.
- Air fry for 15-20 minutes, shaking the basket occasionally, until the chickpeas are crispy and golden.
- Remove from the air fryer and let them cool before serving as a crunchy and protein-packed snack.

Mozzarella Sticks

Ingredients:
- 8 mozzarella sticks, cut in half
- 1/2 cup gluten-free breadcrumbs
- 1/4 cup grated Parmesan cheese
- 1 teaspoon Italian seasoning
- 2 large eggs, beaten
- Marinara sauce, for dipping

Instructions:
- Preheat your air fryer to 400°F (200°C).

- In a shallow bowl, combine the gluten-free breadcrumbs, grated Parmesan cheese, and Italian seasoning.
- Dip each mozzarella stick half into the beaten eggs, allowing any excess to drip off, and then coat it in the breadcrumb mixture.
- Put the coated mozzarella sticks in the air fryer basket in a single layer.
- Air fry for 6-8 minutes until the mozzarella sticks are golden and the cheese is melted.
- Take them out of the air fryer and allow them to cool before serving with marinara sauce.

Crispy Brussels Sprouts

Ingredients:
- 1 pound Brussels sprouts, trimmed and halved
- 2 tablespoons olive oil
- 1 teaspoon garlic powder
- 1/2 teaspoon smoked paprika
- Salt and pepper, to taste

Instructions:

- Preheat your air fryer to 400°F (200°C).
- In a bowl, toss the Brussels sprouts with olive oil, garlic powder, smoked paprika, salt, and pepper until well coated.
- In the air fryer basket, put the seasoned Brussels sprouts.
- Air fry for 15 to 20 minutes, shaking the basket occasionally, until the Brussels sprouts are lightly charred and crispy.
- Remove from the air fryer and serve as a flavorful and healthy appetizer or snack.

Chicken Wings

Ingredients:
- 1 pound chicken wings
- 2 tablespoons olive oil
- 1 teaspoon garlic powder
- 1 teaspoon paprika
- 1/2 teaspoon salt
- 1/4 teaspoon black pepper

- Buffalo sauce or barbecue sauce, for tossing (optional)

Instructions:
- Preheat your air fryer to 400°F (200°C).
- Chicken wings should be thoroughly coated in olive oil, garlic powder, paprika, salt, and black pepper in a bowl.
- The seasoned chicken wings should be placed in the air fryer basket in a single layer.
- Air fry for 20-25 minutes, flipping the wings halfway through, until they are crispy and cooked through.
- If desired, toss the cooked wings in your favorite sauce (such as buffalo or barbecue) before serving.

Sweet Potato Chips

Ingredients:
- 2 medium sweet potatoes
- 2 tablespoons olive oil

- 1 teaspoon paprika
- 1/2 teaspoon garlic powder
- Salt and pepper, to taste

Instructions:

- Preheat your air fryer to 375°F (190°C).
- Cut the sweet potatoes into rounds that are just 1/8 inch thick.
- In a bowl, toss the sweet potato slices with olive oil, paprika, garlic powder, salt, and pepper until well coated.
- Place the seasoned sweet potato slices in a single layer in the air fryer basket.
- Air fry for 12-15 minutes, flipping the slices halfway through, until they are crispy and lightly browned.
- Remove from the air fryer and let them cool before serving as a crunchy gluten-free snack.

CHAPTER FIVE

Sizzling Sensations: Flavorful Gluten-Free Meats and Seafood

Lemon Herb Salmon

Ingredients:

- 2 salmon fillets
- 2 tablespoons olive oil
- 1 tablespoon fresh lemon juice
- 1 teaspoon lemon zest
- 1 teaspoon dried dill
- Salt and pepper, to taste

Instructions:

- Preheat your air fryer to 400°F (200°C).
- In a small bowl, combine the olive oil, lemon juice, lemon zest, dried dill, salt, and pepper.
- Place the salmon fillets on a plate and brush them with the prepared marinade, ensuring both sides are coated.

- The salmon fillets should be transferred to the air fryer basket.
- Air fry for 10-12 minutes, depending on the thickness of the fillets, until the salmon is cooked through and flakes easily with a fork.
- Remove it from the air fryer. Let them rest for a few minutes before serving.

Spicy Chicken Drumsticks

Ingredients:

- 6 chicken drumsticks
- 2 tablespoons olive oil
- 1 teaspoon paprika
- 1/2 teaspoon chili powder
- 1/2 teaspoon garlic powder
- 1/2 teaspoon onion powder
- 1/4 teaspoon cayenne pepper (adjust to taste)
- Salt and pepper, to taste

Instructions:

- Preheat your air fryer to 400°F (200°C).

- In a bowl, combine the olive oil, paprika, chili powder, garlic powder, onion powder, cayenne pepper, salt, and pepper.
- The chicken drumsticks should be dried with a paper towel.
- Coat the drumsticks with the prepared spice mixture, ensuring they are evenly coated.
- The drumsticks should be arranged in a single layer in the air fryer basket.
- Air fry for 25-30 minutes, flipping the drumsticks halfway through, until they are golden brown and the internal temperature reaches 165°F (74°C).
- Before serving, take them out of the air fryer and allow them to rest for a while.

Garlic and Herb Turkey Meatballs

Ingredients:
- 1 pound ground turkey
- 1/4 cup gluten-free breadcrumbs
- 1/4 cup grated Parmesan cheese

- 2 cloves garlic, minced
- 2 teaspoons of freshly chopped herbs, such as thyme, basil, or parsley
- 1 teaspoon dried oregano
- 1/2 teaspoon salt
- 1/4 teaspoon black pepper

Instructions:

- Preheat your air fryer to 375°F (190°C).
- In a mixing bowl, combine the ground turkey, gluten-free breadcrumbs, grated Parmesan cheese, minced garlic, chopped fresh herbs, dried oregano, salt, and black pepper. Mix until well combined.
- Shape the mixture into small meatballs.
- The meatballs should be placed in the air fryer basket in a single layer.
- Air fry for 12-15 minutes, shaking the basket occasionally, until the meatballs are cooked through and browned.

- Remove them from the air fryer, then allow them to cool for a few minutes before serving.

Coconut Shrimp

Ingredients:
- 1 pound large shrimp, peeled and deveined
- 1/2 cup gluten-free breadcrumbs
- 1/2 cup unsweetened shredded coconut
- 2 large eggs, beaten
- Salt and pepper, to taste
- Sauce for dipping (such as mango salsa or sweet chili sauce)

Instructions:
- Preheat your air fryer to 400°F (200°C).
- In a shallow bowl, combine the gluten-free breadcrumbs, shredded coconut, salt, and pepper.

- Dip each shrimp into the beaten eggs, allowing any excess to drip off, and then coat it in the breadcrumb-coconut mixture.
- Place the coated shrimp in the air fryer basket in a single layer.
- Air fry for 8-10 minutes, flipping the shrimp halfway through, until they are crispy and lightly golden.
- Remove from the air fryer and serve hot with your preferred dipping sauce.

Honey Mustard Glazed Pork Chops

Ingredients:
- 2 pork chops
- 2 tablespoons Dijon mustard
- 1 tablespoon honey
- 1 teaspoon minced garlic
- 1/2 teaspoon dried thyme
- Salt and pepper, to taste

Instructions:

- Preheat your air fryer to 400°F (200°C).
- In a small bowl, whisk together the Dijon mustard, honey, minced garlic, dried thyme, salt, and pepper.
- Use a paper towel to pat-dry the pork chops.
- Brush both sides of the pork chops with the honey mustard glaze.
- Put the pork chops in the air fryer basket.
- Air fry for 12-15 minutes, flipping the pork chops halfway through, until they reach an internal temperature of 145°F (63°C).
- Remove the air fryer. Also, allow them to rest for a few minutes before serving.

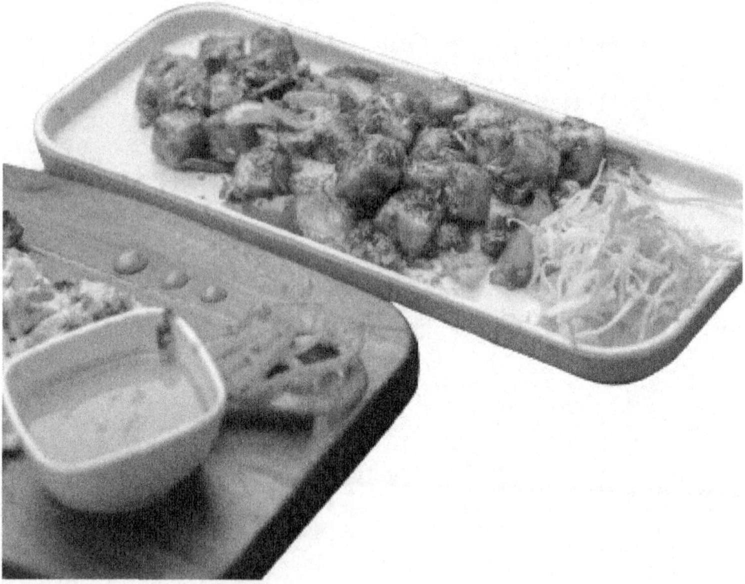

CHAPTER SIX

Veggie Delights: Elevating Gluten-Free Vegetables to New Heights

Roasted Brussels Sprouts

Ingredients:

- 1 pound Brussels sprouts, trimmed and halved
- 2 tablespoons olive oil
- 1 teaspoon garlic powder
- 1/2 teaspoon smoked paprika
- Salt and pepper, to taste

Instructions:

- Preheat your air fryer to 400°F (200°C).
- In a bowl, toss the Brussels sprouts with olive oil, garlic powder, smoked paprika, salt, and pepper until well coated.
- The seasoned Brussels sprouts should be placed in the air fryer basket.

- The Brussels sprouts should be crispy and lightly charred after air-frying them for 15 to 20 minutes while occasionally shaking the basket.
- Remove from the air fryer and serve as a flavorful and healthy side dish.

Zucchini Fries

Ingredients:
- 2 medium zucchini, cut into fry-shaped sticks
- 1/2 cup gluten-free breadcrumbs
- 1/4 cup grated Parmesan cheese
- 1 teaspoon dried Italian seasoning
- 2 large eggs, beaten
- Marinara sauce, for dipping

Instructions:
- Preheat your air fryer to 400°F (200°C).
- In a shallow bowl, combine the gluten-free breadcrumbs, grated Parmesan cheese, and dried Italian seasoning.

- Each zucchini stick should be dipped into the beaten eggs, letting any extra drip off, before getting coated with the breadcrumb mixture.
- Place the coated zucchini sticks in the air fryer basket in a single layer.
- Air fry for 10 to 12 minutes, flipping the sticks halfway through, until they are golden and crispy.
- Remove from the air fryer and serve hot, with marinara sauce for dipping.

Sweet Potato Fries

Ingredients:

- 2 medium sweet potatoes, cut into fry-shaped sticks
- 2 tablespoons olive oil
- 1 teaspoon paprika
- 1/2 teaspoon garlic powder
- Salt and pepper, to taste

Instructions:

- Preheat your air fryer to 400°F (200°C).
- In a bowl, toss the sweet potato sticks with olive oil, paprika, garlic powder, salt, and pepper until well coated.
- Place the seasoned sweet potato sticks in the air fryer basket in a single layer.
- Air fry for 15-20 minutes, shaking the basket occasionally, until the sweet potato fries are crispy and lightly browned.
- Remove from the air fryer and serve as a delicious and healthy side dish or snack.

Parmesan Roasted Cauliflower

Ingredients:
- 1 medium cauliflower head, divided into florets
- 2 tablespoons olive oil
- 1/4 cup grated Parmesan cheese
- 1 teaspoon dried thyme
- 1/2 teaspoon garlic powder
- Salt and pepper, to taste

Instructions:

- Preheat your air fryer to 400°F (200°C).
- In a bowl, toss the cauliflower florets with olive oil, grated Parmesan cheese, dried thyme, garlic powder, salt, and pepper until well coated.
- Place the seasoned cauliflower florets in the air fryer basket.
- Air fry for 12-15 minutes, shaking the basket occasionally, until the cauliflower is tender and golden.
- Remove from the air fryer and serve as a flavorful and nutritious side dish.

Eggplant Chips

Ingredients:

- 1 medium eggplant, thinly sliced into rounds
- 2 tablespoons olive oil
- 1/2 teaspoon dried oregano
- 1/2 teaspoon garlic powder
- Salt and pepper, to taste

Instructions:

- Preheat your air fryer to 375°F (190°C).
- In a bowl, toss the eggplant slices with olive oil, dried oregano, garlic powder, salt, and pepper until well coated.
- Put a single layer of the seasoned eggplant slices in the air fryer basket.
- Air fry for 10-12 minutes, flipping the slices halfway through, until they are crispy and lightly browned.
- Remove from the air fryer and serve as a crunchy and delicious snack.

CHAPTER SEVEN

Comfort Classics Reinvented: Gluten-Free Air Fryer Makeovers

Crispy Cauliflower Buffalo Wings

Ingredients:

- 1 head cauliflower, cut into florets
- 1/2 cup gluten-free flour
- 1/2 cup almond milk
- 1 teaspoon garlic powder
- 1 teaspoon paprika
- 1/2 teaspoon salt
- 1/4 teaspoon black pepper
- 1/4 cup hot sauce
- 2 tablespoons melted vegan butter

Instructions:

- Preheat your air fryer to 400°F (200°C).

- In a bowl, whisk together the gluten-free flour, almond milk, garlic powder, paprika, salt, and black pepper to create a batter.
- Dip each cauliflower floret into the batter, ensuring it is evenly coated, and shake off any excess.
- Put the coated cauliflower florets in a single layer in the air fryer basket.
- Air fry for 15-18 minutes, flipping the florets halfway through, until they are crispy and golden.
- In a separate bowl, whisk together the hot sauce and melted vegan butter to create the buffalo sauce.
- Toss the cooked cauliflower florets in the buffalo sauce until well coated.
- Serve hot with your choice of dipping sauce, such as vegan ranch or blue cheese dressing.

Quinoa-Crusted Chicken Tenders

Ingredients:

- 1 pound boneless, skinless chicken tenders
- 1/2 cup cooked quinoa
- 1/4 cup gluten-free breadcrumbs
- 1/4 cup grated Parmesan cheese
- 1 teaspoon garlic powder
- 1/2 teaspoon paprika
- Salt and pepper, to taste
- 2 eggs, beaten

Instructions:

- Preheat your air fryer to 400°F (200°C).
- In a shallow bowl, combine the cooked quinoa, gluten-free breadcrumbs, grated Parmesan cheese, garlic powder, paprika, salt, and pepper.
- Dip each chicken tender into the beaten eggs, allowing any excess to drip off, and then coat it in the quinoa mixture.
- The coated chicken tenders should be placed in the air fryer basket in a single layer.

- Air fry for 12-15 minutes, flipping the tenders halfway through, until they are crispy and cooked through.
- They should be removed from the air fryer. Let them rest for a few minutes before serving.
- Serve with your favorite gluten-free dipping sauce, such as honey mustard or barbecue sauce.

Baked Zucchini Fries

Ingredients:
- 2 medium zucchini, cut into fry-shaped sticks
- 1/2 cup gluten-free breadcrumbs
- 1/4 cup grated Parmesan cheese
- 1/2 teaspoon garlic powder
- 1/2 teaspoon dried Italian seasoning
- Salt and pepper, to taste
- 2 large eggs, beaten

Instructions:
- Preheat your air fryer to 400°F (200°C).

- In a shallow bowl, combine the gluten-free breadcrumbs, grated Parmesan cheese, garlic powder, dried Italian seasoning, salt, and pepper.
- Each zucchini stick should be dipped into the beaten eggs, letting any extra drip off, before it is coated with the breadcrumb mixture.
- Place the coated zucchini sticks in the air fryer basket in a single layer.
- To get the sticks crispy and golden, air fried them for 10 to 12 minutes, flipping the sticks halfway through.
- Remove from the air fryer and serve hot with marinara sauce or a yogurt-based dip.

Sweet Potato Tots

Ingredients:
- 2 medium sweet potatoes, peeled and grated
- 1/4 cup almond flour
- 2 tablespoons coconut flour

- 1 teaspoon garlic powder
- 1/2 teaspoon paprika
- Salt and pepper, to taste
- 2 tablespoons olive oil

Instructions:

- Preheat your air fryer to 400°F (200°C).
- Place the grated sweet potatoes in a clean kitchen towel and squeeze out any excess moisture.
- In a bowl, combine the squeezed sweet potatoes, almond flour, coconut flour, garlic powder, paprika, salt, pepper, and olive oil.
- Form the mixture into small tot shapes and place them in the air fryer basket in a single layer.
- Air fry for 12-15 minutes, flipping the tots halfway through, until they are crispy and golden.
- Remove from the air fryer and let them cool slightly before serving.

- Enjoy the sweet potato tots on their own or serve them with a dipping sauce of your choice.

Eggplant Parmesan

Ingredients:
- 1 medium eggplant, sliced into rounds that are 1/2 inch thick.
- 1 cup gluten-free breadcrumbs
- 1/4 cup grated Parmesan cheese
- 1 teaspoon dried Italian seasoning
- 1/2 teaspoon garlic powder
- Salt and pepper, to taste
- 2 large eggs, beaten
- 1 cup marinara sauce
- 1 cup shredded mozzarella cheese
- Fresh basil leaves, for garnish

Instructions:
- Preheat your air fryer to 400°F (200°C).
- In a shallow bowl, combine the gluten-free breadcrumbs, grated Parmesan cheese, dried

Italian seasoning, garlic powder, salt, and pepper.
- Dip each eggplant round into the beaten eggs, allowing any excess to drip off, and then coat it in the breadcrumb mixture.
- Place the coated eggplant rounds in the air fryer basket in a single layer.
- Air fry for 10-12 minutes, flipping the rounds halfway through, until they are crispy and golden.
- Take out of the air fryer, then place aside.
- Spread a thin layer of marinara sauce in a baking dish.
- Arrange the cooked eggplant rounds on top of the sauce.
- Spoon additional marinara sauce over each round and sprinkle with shredded mozzarella cheese.
- Place the dish in the air fryer and air fry for an additional 5-7 minutes, or until the cheese is melted and bubbly.

- Remove from the air fryer and let it cool slightly before serving.
- Garnish with fresh basil leaves and serve as a delicious gluten-free version of eggplant Parmesan.

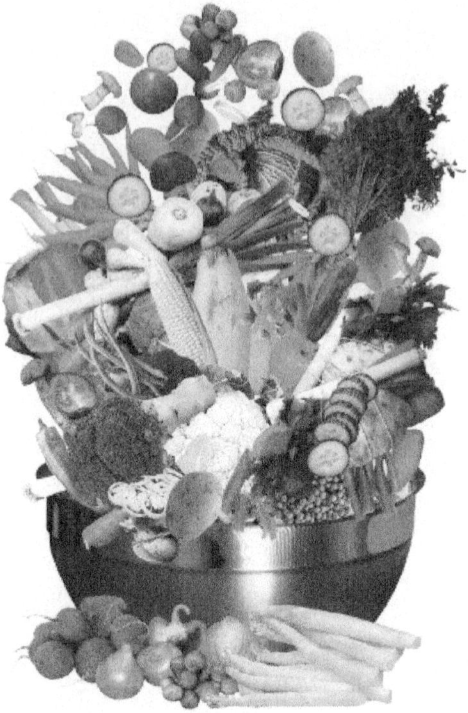

CHAPTER EIGHT

International Flavors: Exploring Gluten-Free Air Fryer Recipes from Around the World

Korean-Style Chicken Wings

Ingredients:

- 1 pound chicken wings
- 2 tablespoons gluten-free soy sauce
- 1 tablespoon honey
- 1 tablespoon sesame oil
- 1 teaspoon minced garlic
- 1 teaspoon grated ginger
- 1/2 teaspoon gochugaru (Korean red pepper flakes)
- 1/4 teaspoon black pepper
- Toasted sesame seeds, for garnish
- Sliced green onions, for garnish

Instructions:

- Preheat your air fryer to 400°F (200°C).
- In a bowl, whisk together the gluten-free soy sauce, honey, sesame oil, minced garlic, grated ginger, gochugaru, and black pepper to create a marinade.
- Place the chicken wings in a zip-top bag and pour the marinade over them. Seal the bag and shake to coat the wings evenly.
- Let the wings marinate in the refrigerator for at least 30 minutes, or up to overnight for more flavor.
- Place the marinated chicken wings in the air fryer basket in a single layer.
- Air fry for 20-25 minutes, flipping the wings halfway through, until they are crispy and cooked through.
- Remove from the air fryer and garnish with toasted sesame seeds and sliced green onions.
- Serve hot as a delicious and flavorful appetizer.

Mexican-Style Stuffed Peppers

Ingredients:
- 4 large bell peppers, tops and seeds removed, any color.
- 1 pound ground beef or turkey
- 1 cup cooked quinoa
- 1 cup black beans, rinsed and drained
- 1/2 cup corn kernels
- 1/2 cup diced tomatoes
- 1/4 cup chopped fresh cilantro
- 1 teaspoon chili powder
- 1/2 teaspoon cumin
- 1/2 teaspoon garlic powder
- Salt and pepper, to taste
- Shredded cheddar or dairy-free cheese, for topping
- Sliced avocado, for garnish

Instructions:
- Preheat your air fryer to 375°F (190°C).

- In a skillet, cook the ground beef or turkey until browned and cooked through. Drain any excess fat.
- In a large bowl, combine the cooked ground meat, cooked quinoa, black beans, corn kernels, diced tomatoes, chopped cilantro, chili powder, cumin, garlic powder, salt, and pepper. Mix well.
- Stuff the mixture into the hollowed-out bell peppers, pressing it down firmly.
- The stuffed peppers should be placed in the air fryer basket.
- Air fry for 20-25 minutes, or until the peppers are tender and the filling is heated through.
- Sprinkle shredded cheddar or dairy-free cheese on top of each pepper and air fry for an additional 2-3 minutes, or until the cheese is melted and bubbly.
- Remove from the air fryer and let them cool slightly before serving.

- Garnish with sliced avocado and serve as a delicious and satisfying main course.

Thai-Style Coconut Shrimp

Ingredients:
- 1 pound large shrimp, peeled and deveined
- 1/2 cup gluten-free flour
- 1/2 cup shredded coconut
- 1/2 teaspoon garlic powder
- 1/2 teaspoon paprika
- Salt and pepper, to taste
- 2 eggs, beaten
- Sweet chili sauce, for dipping

Instructions:

Preheat your air fryer to 400°F (200°C).

In a shallow bowl, combine the gluten-free flour, shredded coconut, garlic powder, paprika, salt, and pepper.

Dip each shrimp into the beaten eggs, allowing any excess to drip off, and then coat it in the coconut mixture.

- Arrange the coated shrimp in a single layer in the air fryer basket.
- Air fry for 10-12 minutes, flipping the shrimp halfway through, until they are golden and crispy.
- Remove from the air fryer and let them cool slightly before serving.
- Serve the coconut shrimp with sweet chili sauce for dipping, adding a touch of Thai-inspired flavor to your meal.

Indian-Style Vegetable Samosas

Ingredients:
- 1 cup mashed potatoes
- 1/2 cup peas
- 1/4 cup finely chopped onion
- 1/4 cup finely chopped carrots

- 1 teaspoon minced ginger
- 1 teaspoon minced garlic
- 1 teaspoon curry powder
- 1/2 teaspoon garam masala
- 1/4 teaspoon turmeric
- Salt and pepper, to taste
- Gluten-free spring roll wrappers
- Olive oil, for brushing

Instructions:

- Preheat your air fryer to 375°F (190°C).
- In a pan, sauté the onions, carrots, ginger, and garlic until the vegetables are tender.
- Add the mashed potatoes, peas, curry powder, garam masala, turmeric, salt, and pepper to the pan. Mix well and cook for an additional 2-3 minutes.
- Cut the spring roll wrappers into small squares.
- Place a spoonful of the vegetable filling in the center of each wrapper.

- Fold the wrapper diagonally to form a triangle and seal the edges with water.
- Brush the samosas with olive oil to promote crispiness.
- Samosas should be arranged in a single layer in the air fryer basket.
- Air fry for 10-12 minutes, flipping the samosas halfway through, until they are golden brown and crispy.

- Remove from the air fryer and let them cool slightly before serving.
- Serve the vegetable samosas as a delicious appetizer or snack, and pair them with your favorite chutney or dipping sauce.

Japanese-Style Teriyaki Salmon

Ingredients:
- 2 salmon fillets
- 1/4 cup gluten-free teriyaki sauce
- 1 tablespoon gluten-free soy sauce

- 1 tablespoon honey or maple syrup
- 1 teaspoon grated ginger
- 1 teaspoon minced garlic
- Sesame seeds, for garnish
- Sliced green onions, for garnish

Instructions:

- Preheat your air fryer to 400°F (200°C).
- In a bowl, whisk together the gluten-free teriyaki sauce, gluten-free soy sauce, honey or maple syrup, grated ginger, and minced garlic to create the marinade.
- Place the salmon fillets in a zip-top bag and pour the marinade over them. Seal the bag and let the salmon marinate for at least 30 minutes in the refrigerator.
- Place the marinated salmon fillets in the air fryer basket.
- Air fry for 10-12 minutes, depending on the thickness of the fillets, until the salmon is cooked through and flakes easily with a fork.

- Remove from the air fryer and allow them some time to cool.
- Use sesame seeds and thinly sliced green onions to garnish.
- Serve the teriyaki salmon with steamed rice or vegetables for a delicious and healthy Japanese-inspired meal.

CHAPTER NINE

Sweet Indulgences: Irresistible Gluten-Free Desserts and Treats

Cinnamon Sugar Donut Holes

Ingredients:
- 1 cup gluten-free flour blend
- 1/4 cup granulated sugar
- 1 teaspoon baking powder
- 1/2 teaspoon ground cinnamon
- 1/4 teaspoon salt
- Any non-dairy milk, or 1/2 cup of unsweetened almond milk
- 2 tablespoons coconut oil, melted
- 1 teaspoon vanilla extract
- 2 tablespoons powdered sugar (for dusting)

Instructions:
- Preheat your air fryer to 350°F (175°C).

- In a bowl, whisk together the gluten-free flour, granulated sugar, baking powder, cinnamon, and salt.
- The dry ingredients should be combined with the melted coconut oil, almond milk, and vanilla essence. Stir until well combined and a smooth batter forms.
- Drop spoonfuls of the batter into the air fryer basket, making small donut holes.
- Air fry for 8-10 minutes, or until the donut holes are golden brown and cooked through.
- They should be removed from the air fryer and let them cool slightly.
- Dust the cinnamon sugar donut holes with powdered sugar.
- Serve them warm as a delightful gluten-free treat.

Berry Crumble Bars

Ingredients:

- 1 cup gluten-free oats

- 1/2 cup almond flour
- 1/4 cup coconut sugar
- 1/4 teaspoon ground cinnamon
- 1/4 cup coconut oil, melted
- 1/4 cup pure maple syrup
- 1 cup of mixed berries, like blackberries, raspberries, or blueberries
- 1 tablespoon lemon juice

Instructions:

- Preheat your air fryer to 350°F (175°C).
- In a bowl, combine the gluten-free oats, almond flour, coconut sugar, and ground cinnamon.
- Add the melted coconut oil and maple syrup to the mixture, and stir until well combined and crumbly.
- Set aside 1/4 cup of the mixture for the topping.
- Press the remaining mixture into the bottom of a greased air fryer-safe baking dish.

- In a separate bowl, toss the mixed berries with lemon juice.
- Spread the berry mixture evenly over the oat mixture in the baking dish.
- Sprinkle the reserved crumb mixture on top of the berries.
- Place the baking dish in the air fryer and air fry for 15-20 minutes, or until the topping is golden brown and the berries are bubbly.
- Remove from the air fryer and let it cool completely before cutting into bars.
- Serve the berry crumble bars as a scrumptious gluten-free dessert.

Chocolate Chip Cookies

Ingredients:
- 1 cup gluten-free flour blend
- 1/2 teaspoon baking soda
- 1/4 teaspoon salt
- 1/2 cup coconut oil, melted
- 1/2 cup coconut sugar

- 1/4 cup granulated sugar
- 1 teaspoon vanilla extract
- 1 egg
- 1/2 cup dairy-free chocolate chips

Instructions:

- Preheat your air fryer to 350°F (175°C).
- Mix the salt, baking soda, and gluten-free flour in a bowl.
- In a separate bowl, cream together the melted coconut oil, coconut sugar, granulated sugar, vanilla extract, and egg until well combined.
- Till a dough forms, gradually combine the dry components with the moist ones.
- Fold in the dairy-free chocolate chips.
- Drop spoonfuls of the cookie dough onto a greased air fryer basket, spacing them apart.
- Air fry for 8-10 minutes, or until the cookies are golden brown around the edges.
- Remove from the air fryer and let them cool on a wire rack.

- Enjoy these delicious gluten-free chocolate chip cookies with a glass of milk or your favorite hot beverage.

Apple Hand Pies

Ingredients:

- 2 cups gluten-free flour blend
- 1/2 teaspoon xanthan gum (if your flour blend doesn't contain it)
- 1/4 teaspoon salt
- 1/2 cup coconut oil, solid
- 1/4 cup cold water
- 2 apples, peeled, cored, and diced
- 2 tablespoons coconut sugar
- 1/2 teaspoon ground cinnamon
- 1/4 teaspoon ground nutmeg
- 1/4 teaspoon ground cloves
- 1 tablespoon lemon juice
- 1 tablespoon cornstarch

Instructions:

- Preheat your air fryer to 375°F (190°C).
- In a bowl, whisk together the gluten-free flour, xanthan gum (if needed), and salt.
- Until the flour mixture resembles coarse crumbs, cut in the solid coconut oil.
- Gradually add the cold water, mixing until a dough forms. Shape the dough into a ball.
- Roll out the dough to a thickness of about 1/8 inch on a surface lightly dusted with flour..
- Using a round cutter, cut out circles from the rolled dough.
- In a separate bowl, toss the diced apples with coconut sugar, ground cinnamon, ground nutmeg, ground cloves, lemon juice, and cornstarch until well coated.
- Place a spoonful of the apple mixture onto the center of each dough circle.
- Fold the dough over the filling to create a half-moon shape, and press the edges to seal.
- Place the hand pies in the air fryer basket in a single layer.

- Air fry for 10-12 minutes, or until the hand pies are golden brown and the apples are tender.
- Remove from the air fryer and let them cool slightly before serving.
- Indulge in these delightful gluten-free apple hand pies as a sweet treat.

Vanilla Glazed Donuts

Ingredients:
- 1 cup gluten-free flour blend
- 1/4 cup coconut sugar
- 1 teaspoon baking powder
- 1/4 teaspoon salt
- 1/4 cup unsweetened almond milk (or any non-dairy milk)
- 2 tablespoons coconut oil, melted
- 1 teaspoon vanilla extract
- For the glaze:
- 1 cup powdered sugar
- 2 tablespoons of unsweetened almond (or other non-dairy) milk

- 1/2 teaspoon vanilla extract

Instructions:
- Preheat your air fryer to 350°F (175°C).
- In a bowl, whisk together the gluten-free flour, coconut sugar, baking powder, and salt.
- The dry ingredients should be combined with the melted coconut oil, almond milk, and vanilla essence. Stir until well combined and a smooth batter forms.
- Drop spoonfuls of the batter into a greased air fryer donut pan, filling each cavity about three-quarters full.
- Air fry for 8-10 minutes, or until the donuts are golden brown and cooked through.
- Remove from the air fryer and give them some time to cool.
- In a separate bowl, whisk together the powdered sugar, almond milk, and vanilla extract until smooth to create the glaze.

- Dip the cooled donuts into the glaze, allowing any excess to drip off.
- The glazed donuts should be placed on a wire rack to set.
- Serve these delightful gluten-free vanilla glazed donuts as a heavenly dessert or sweet snack.

CHAPTER TEN

Bonus: Tips, Tricks, and Modifications for Gluten-Free Air Frying Success

Gluten-free air frying opens up a world of delicious possibilities for individuals with dietary restrictions. With the right techniques and modifications, you can achieve crispy and flavorful results that rival traditional fried dishes. Whether you're new to gluten-free air frying or looking to enhance your skills, here are some valuable tips, tricks, and modifications to ensure gluten-free air frying success.

Choose Gluten-Free Ingredients:
To create gluten-free dishes in the air fryer, it's essential to start with gluten-free ingredients. Check labels carefully to ensure that all components of your recipe, including flours, seasonings, and sauces, are free from gluten. Look for products that are certified

gluten-free or labeled as suitable for those with celiac disease or gluten intolerance.

Experiment with Gluten-Free Flours:
Gluten-free flours vary in their texture and taste, so it's worth exploring different options to find the ones that work best for your recipes. Some popular choices include rice flour, almond flour, coconut flour, and chickpea flour. Blending different flours can help achieve a more balanced and satisfying result. Additionally, consider adding a small amount of xanthan gum to improve texture and binding in gluten-free batters and doughs.

Adjust Cooking Time and Temperature:
Gluten-free foods may cook faster than their gluten-containing counterparts in the air fryer. Keep a close eye on the cooking process and adjust the recommended cooking time and temperature as needed. Start with the suggested guidelines, but rely on visual cues such as color, crispness, and internal

temperature to determine when your food is perfectly cooked.

Use Oil or Cooking Spray:
While air frying reduces the need for excessive oil, adding a small amount can enhance the texture and flavor of gluten-free dishes. Lightly coat your ingredients with cooking spray or brush them with a thin layer of oil before air frying. This helps create a crisp exterior while maintaining moisture inside.

Incorporate Gluten-Free Coatings and Batters:
To achieve a satisfying crunch on your gluten-free dishes, experiment with different coatings and batters. Gluten-free alternatives such as rice flour, cornmeal, or crushed gluten-free cereal can provide a crispy texture. Consider using gluten-free breadcrumbs or panko for breaded items, and try incorporating flavorful herbs and spices to enhance the taste.

Optimize Seasoning and Flavorings:

Gluten-free dishes can sometimes lack the depth of flavor that gluten-containing counterparts provide. To enhance the taste of your gluten-free air-fried meals, experiment with various seasonings, spices, and marinades. Fresh herbs, citrus zest, garlic, onion powder, and smoked paprika can add complexity and richness to your dishes.

Prevent Cross-Contamination:

If you have a gluten intolerance or celiac disease, it's crucial to prevent cross-contamination when using shared kitchen appliances like air fryers. Consider using a separate air fryer or using parchment paper or silicone mats to create a barrier between gluten-containing and gluten-free foods. Clean the air fryer thoroughly before each use to remove any potential traces of gluten.

Experiment with Alternative Ingredients:

Embrace the versatility of gluten-free air frying by exploring alternative ingredients. For example, instead of using traditional breadcrumbs, try crushed gluten-free crackers or nuts for a crunchy coating. Cauliflower, zucchini, and sweet potatoes can be transformed into delicious gluten-free fries or vegetable chips. Be creative and adapt your favorite recipes to accommodate gluten-free ingredients.

Adapt Recipes to Dietary Needs:
Gluten-free air frying opens doors for individuals with various dietary needs. With simple modifications, you can cater to other dietary preferences or restrictions, such as vegan or dairy-free. Substitute dairy products with non-dairy alternatives and adjust seasoning accordingly. Experiment with plant-based proteins, tofu, or tempeh to create satisfying gluten-free and vegan dishes.

Embrace the Learning Process:

Mastering gluten-free air frying takes time and experimentation. Embrace the learning process and don't be discouraged by the occasional trial and error. Keep track of your modifications, note the successful adaptations, and learn from any challenges you encounter. With persistence and creativity, you'll develop your own repertoire of gluten-free air-fried recipes.

In conclusion, achieving gluten-free air frying success requires a combination of careful ingredient selection, modifications, and technique adjustments. By incorporating these tips, tricks, and modifications into your cooking routine, you'll be able to enjoy a wide range of delicious gluten-free dishes that are crispy, flavorful, and satisfying. Happy air frying!

CONCLUSION

In conclusion, the Gluten-Free Air Fryer Cookbook opens up a world of culinary possibilities for individuals seeking delicious and gluten-free meals. Throughout this cookbook, we have explored a diverse range of recipes, tips, and techniques to help you navigate the world of gluten-free air frying with confidence.

From breakfast to desserts, appetizers to main courses, we have showcased the versatility of the air fryer in creating gluten-free dishes that are both flavorful and satisfying. With the right ingredients, proper techniques, and a little creativity, you can enjoy the crispy textures and delicious flavors you crave, all while adhering to your gluten-free lifestyle.

We have provided you with a variety of recipes, ranging from classic favorites with a gluten-free twist to innovative creations that showcase international flavors. Each recipe has been carefully crafted to ensure optimal taste and texture, while also taking into consideration the unique requirements of a gluten-free diet.

Throughout this cookbook, we have shared valuable tips, tricks, and troubleshooting advice to help you achieve gluten-free air frying success. From ingredient selection to cooking time adjustments, these expert insights will empower you to create culinary masterpieces with ease.

We hope that this cookbook has inspired you to embrace the world of gluten-free air frying and explore new horizons in your kitchen. Whether you are new to gluten-free cooking or a seasoned pro, we believe that these recipes will satisfy your cravings and nourish your body.

Remember, the key to successful gluten-free air frying lies in experimentation, adaptation, and personalization. You are free to modify the recipes to suit your taste preferences and dietary needs. Let your creativity soar as you discover new flavor combinations and adapt your favorite dishes to the gluten-free air fryer lifestyle.

Thank you for embarking on this gluten-free air-frying journey with us. We hope that the Gluten-Free Air Fryer Cookbook becomes your trusted companion in the kitchen, inspiring you to create delicious, gluten-free meals that bring joy and satisfaction to your table. **Happy Air Frying!**

Weekly Meal Planner

Monday

Tuesday

Wednesday

Thursday

Friday

Saturday

Sunday

Notes

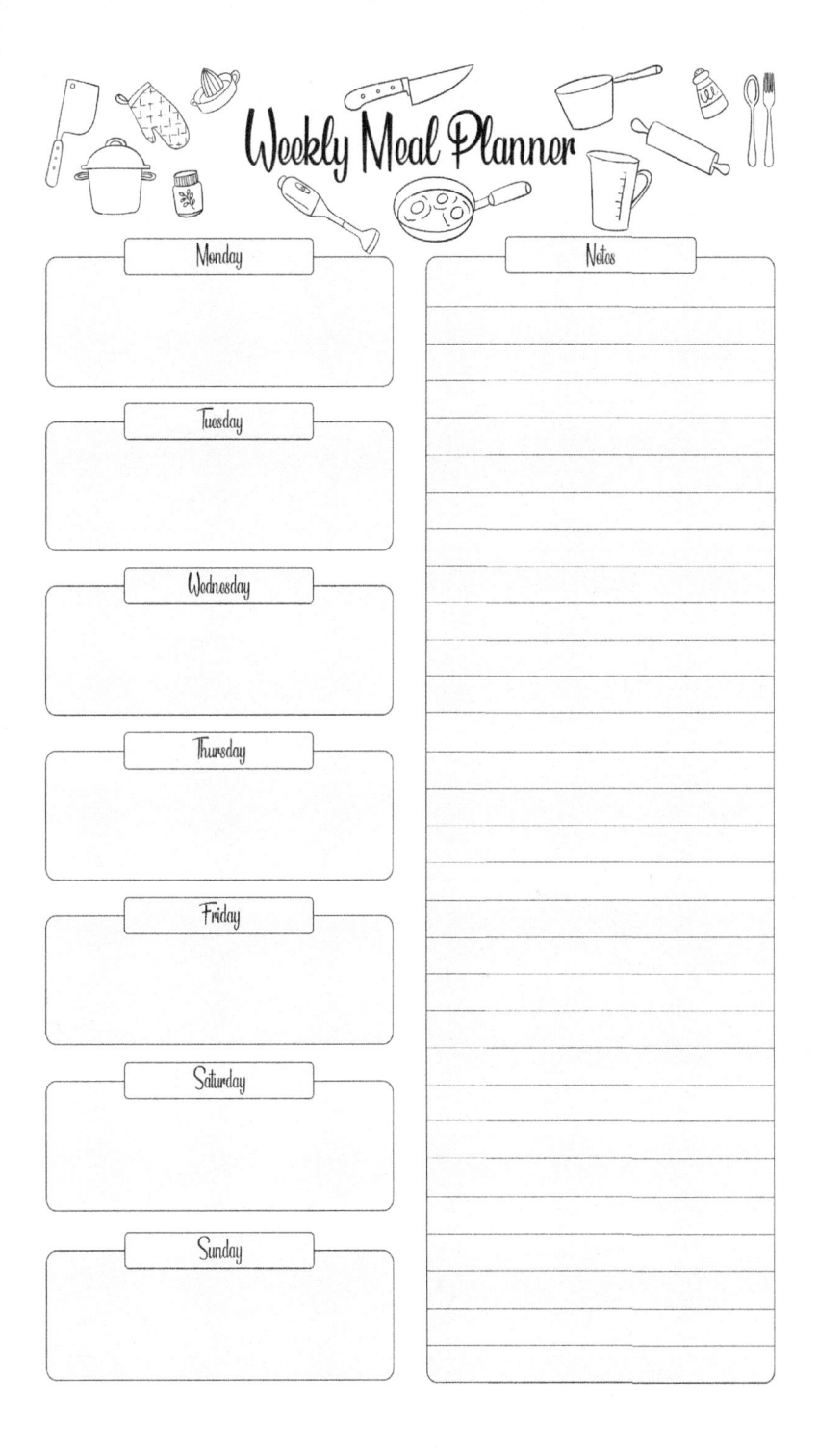

Weekly Meal Planner

Monday

Tuesday

Wednesday

Thursday

Friday

Saturday

Sunday

Notes

Weekly Meal Planner

Monday

Tuesday

Wednesday

Thursday

Friday

Saturday

Sunday

Notes

Weekly Meal Planner

Monday

Tuesday

Wednesday

Thursday

Friday

Saturday

Sunday

Notes

Weekly Meal Planner

Monday

Tuesday

Wednesday

Thursday

Friday

Saturday

Sunday

Notes

Weekly Meal Planner

Monday

Tuesday

Wednesday

Thursday

Friday

Saturday

Sunday

Notes

Weekly Meal Planner

Monday

Tuesday

Wednesday

Thursday

Friday

Saturday

Sunday

Notes

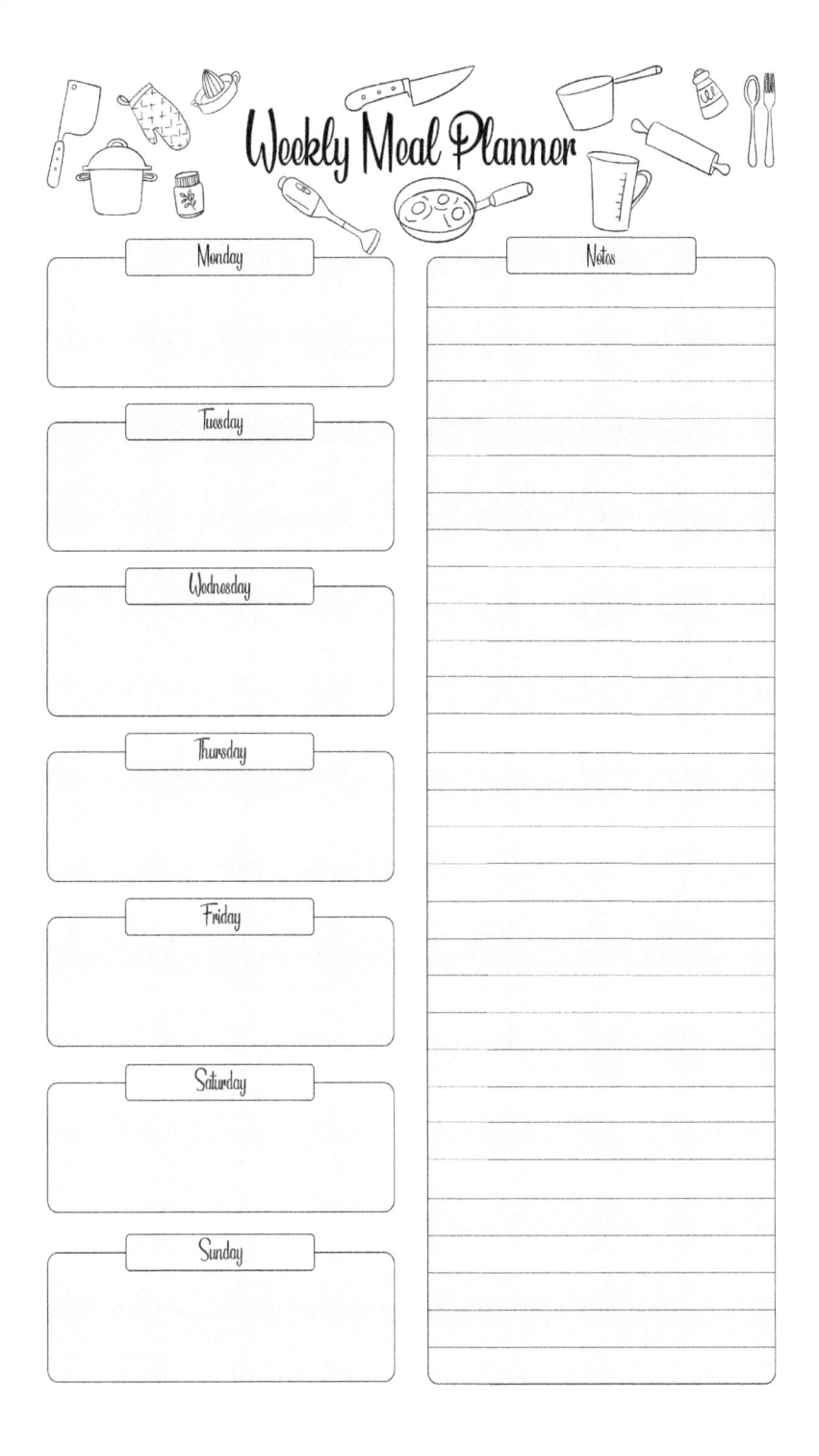

Weekly Meal Planner

Monday

Tuesday

Wednesday

Thursday

Friday

Saturday

Sunday

Notes

Weekly Meal Planner

Monday

Tuesday

Wednesday

Thursday

Friday

Saturday

Sunday

Notes

Weekly Meal Planner

Monday

Tuesday

Wednesday

Thursday

Friday

Saturday

Sunday

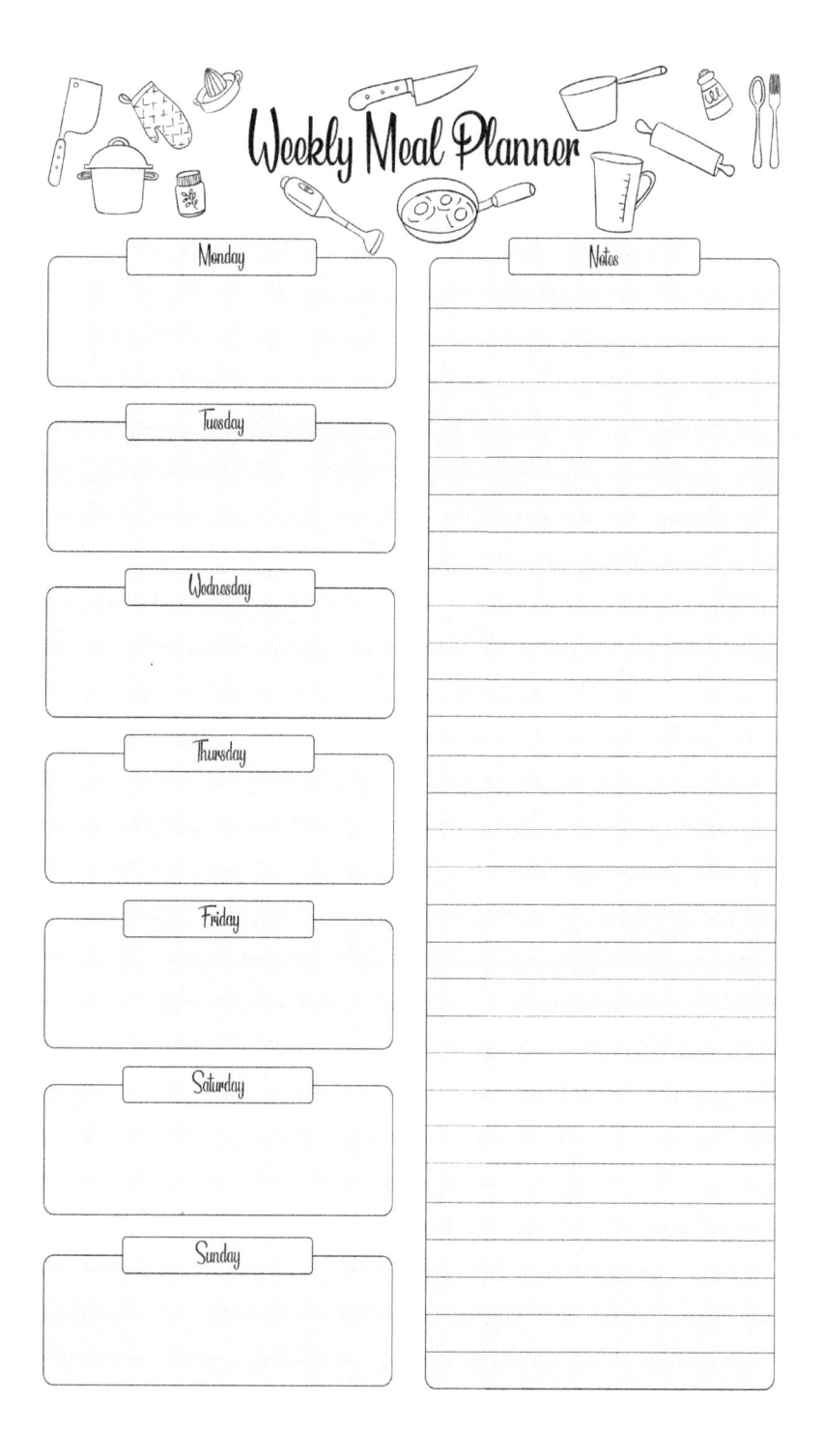

Notes

Printed in Great Britain
by Amazon